Dr. Knucklehead's Knock-Knocks

by Chris Tait

Illustrated by Lance Lekander

Sterling Publishing Co., Inc.
New York

For Henry and Gabriel, the brothers chub

Design by Lucy Wilner

Library of Congress Cataloging-in-Publication Data

Tait, Chris.
  Dr. Knucklehead's knock-knocks / Chris Tait ; illustrated by Lance Lekander.
    p. cm.
  Includes index.
  ISBN 1-4027-2546-9
  1. Knock-knock jokes. 2. Wit and humor, Juvenile. I. Title: Doctor
Knucklehead's knock-knocks. II. Title.

PN6231.K55T35 2005
818'.602—dc22
2005010857

10 9 8 7 6 5

Published in paperback in 2007 by Sterling Publishing Co., Inc.
387 Park Avenue South, New York, NY 10016
© 2005 by Chris Tait
Distributed in Canada by Sterling Publishing
c/o Canadian Manda Group, 165 Dufferin Street
Toronto, Ontario, Canada M6K 3H6
Distributed in the United Kingdom by GMC Distribution Services
Castle Place, 166 High Street, Lewes, East Sussex, England BN7 1XU
Distributed in Australia by Capricorn Link (Australia) Pty. Ltd.
P.O. Box 704, Windsor, NSW 2756, Australia

Sterling ISBN-13: 978-1-4027-0894-7 Hardcover
        ISBN-10: 1-4027-0894-7
        ISBN-13: 978-1-4027-2546-3 Paperback
        ISBN-10: 1-4027-2546-9

For information about custom editions, special sales, premium and
corporate purchases, please contact Sterling Special Sales
Department at 800-805-5489 or specialsales@sterlingpub.com.

Contents

Introduction

Dr. Knucklehead, Knock-Knock Know-It-All, speaks.

The knock-knock joke is as old as the door—maybe older. Who knows? There may have been knock-knock jokes in caves.

> Knock-knock!
> Who's there?
> Urg!
> Urg who?
> Urg you, let me in!

It loses something in the translation, but you can imagine the shaggy caveperson laughter, can't you? In any case, one thing is sure—the knock-knock joke is a classic art form, more important than painting.

Master the great knock-knock and you'll always have a good time. But don't just read the ones in this book. Sure, they're the best knock-knock jokes ever written. But by the time you finish reading this book, they'll be a few months old. Practically ancient by joke standards. So make up your own. You don't have to be a professional. Hey, I'm not really a doctor. I just play one in this book. So go on . . .

Knock-knock!

1 * Knock-Knocks on the Loose

A good knock-knock is only as good as the teller. So remember, when you're telling your friends knock-knocks, be sure to ham it up. And speaking of our little piggy friends, this first section of knock-knocks is all about the wild and woolly world of the animal kingdom. So, purrrfect your purrformance and make your friends roar with laughter....

Knock-knock!
Who's there?
Asp!
Asp who?
Asp me no questions,
I'll tell you no lies!

Knock-knock!
Who's there?
Barked!
Barked who?
Barked my car in the middle
of the road—let's go!

Knock-knock!
Who's there?
Bee hive!
Bee hive who?
Bee hive yourself and
let me in!

Knock-knock!
  Who's there?
Bison!
  Bison who?
Bison—we'll see you when
you get back from school!

Knock-knock!
  Who's there?
Burro!
  Burro who?
Burro a cup of sugar from you?

Knock-knock!
  Who's there?
Camel!
  Camel who?
Camel be mad if we don't get going!

Knock-knock!
  Who's there?
Canary!
  Canary who?
Canary and I come in for
a minute?

Knock-knock!
Who's there?
Canter!
Canter who?
Canter parents just drive her over here to play?

Knock-knock!
Who's there?
Cat!
Cat who?
Cat talk right now; I hab a cold!

Knock-knock!
Who's there?
Foal!
Foal who?
Foal me once, but you can't foal me again!

Knock-knock!
  Who's there?
Feline!
  Feline who?
Feline any better since
your fever broke?

Knock-knock!
  Who's there?
Gallop!
  Gallop who?
Gallop the road said you
had some pie to share!

Knock-knock!
  Who's there?
Fleece!
  Fleece who?
Fleece live on dirty dogs!

Knock-knock!
  Who's there?
Giraffe!
  Giraffe who?
Giraffe 'ter me,
I can tell!

Knock-knock!
  Who's there?
Gopher!
  Gopher who?
Gopher the gold and be
happy with the silver—
that's what I say!

Knock-knock!
  Who's there?
Gorilla!
  Gorilla who?
Gorilla cheese
is my favorite
for lunch!

Knock-knock!
  Who's there?
Iguana!
  Iguana who?
Iguana know where you heard
all these knock-knock jokes!

Knock-knock!
  Who's there?
Lion!
  Lion who?
Lion out here is just
making me cold!

Knock-knock!
  Who's there?
Lizard!
  Lizard who?
Lizard you were having a
party and she invited me!

Knock-knock!
  Who's there?
Ostrich!
  Ostrich who?
Ostrich and ostrich, but
I'm still stiff!

Knock-knock!
  Who's there?
Owl!
  Owl who?
Owl be seeing you!

Knock-knock!
  Who's there?
Panther!
  Panther who?
Panther falling down—open that door now!

Knock-knock!
  Who's there?
Parrot!
  Parrot who?
Parrot least is better than just one!

Knock-knock!
  Who's there?
Pup!
  Pup who?
Pup goes the weasel—
that's who!

{
Knock-knock!
  Who's there?
Rabbit!
  Rabbit who?
  Rabbit up—I'll take it!
}

Knock-knock
  Who's there?
Raptor!
  Raptor who?
Raptor arms around
me—she loves me!

Knock-knock!
  Who's there?
Rat!
  Rat who?
Rat-a-tat. I'm knocking
on your door!

Knock-knock!
  Who's there?
Reindeer!
  Reindeer who?
Reindeer. Looks like
we'll have to have the
picnic another day!

Knock-knock!
  Who's there?
Saddle!
  Saddle who?
Saddle I have to miss
your party!

Knock-knock!
  Who's there?
Spider!
  Spider who?
Spider from across the
street. Is she still home?

Knock-knock!
  Who's there?
Terrace!
  Terrace who?
Terrace a spider on my
shoulder—get it off!

Knock-knock!
    Who's there?
Toucan!
    Toucan who?
Toucan play at this game,
my friend!

Knock-knock!
    Who's there?
Viper!
    Viper who?
Viper feet before you
walk inside the house!

2 * What's in a Name?

As everyone knows, the knock-knock is based on the art of surprise and repetition. The more you hear a name, the less you think of it as a word. But every name has the potential to be misheard as a word or, even better, as two words. This section shows you how to have fun with names. You'll find names you recognize as well as new ones. Feel free to make up knock-knocks with made-up names. Or just have fun making them up with your friends' names.

Knock-knock!
  Who's there?
Adam!
  Adam who?
Adam is what they use to keep all the water in!

Knock-knock!
  Who's there?
Albion!
  Albion who?
Albion the front porch!

Knock-knock!
   Who's there?
Alfie!
   Alfie who?
Alfie better when you
let me in!

Knock-knock!
   Who's there?
Alfred!
   Alfred who?
Alfred ever talks about
is fishing!

Knock-knock!
   Who's there?
Alice!
   Alice who?
Alice not lost, my friend!

Knock-knock!
   Who's there?
Amanda!
   Amanda who?
Amanda help out around the
house would be nice!

Knock-knock!
   Who's there?
Amos!
   Amos who?
Amos be going; I
can't wait around!

Knock-knock!
   Who's there?
Arnott!
   Arnott who?
Arnott you the same guy
who just asked me that?

Knock-knock!
  Who's there?
Arthur!
  Arthur who?
Arthur any more chocolates?
They were delicious!

Knock-knock!
  Who's there?
Bertha!
  Bertha who?
Bertha baby is a great
event!

Knock-knock!
  Who's there?
Blaine!
  Blaine who?
"Blaine drops keep
falling on my head . . ."

Knock-knock!
  Who's there?
Brad!
  Brad who?
Brad dog! No cookie!

Knock-knock!
  Who's there?
Brett!
  Brett who?
Brett you can't guess!

Knock-knock!
  Who's there?
Cameron!
  Cameron who?
Cameron I are going to
take some great pictures!

Knock-knock!
  Who's there?
Camus!
  Camus who?
Camus, but horses whinny!

Knock-knock!
  Who's there?
Carson!
  Carson who?
Carson the freeway
drive too quickly!

Knock-knock!
  Who's there?
Celeste!
  Celeste who?
Celeste time I'm going to tell you,
so listen up!

Knock-knock!
  Who's there?
Donna!
  Donna who?
Donna take any
wooden nickels!

Knock-knock!
  Who's there?
Eli!
  Eli who?
Eli to me—he say you
know who I am!

Knock-knock!
  Who's there?
Eileen!
  Eileen who?
Eileen on your doorbell
for a long time before
you came out!

Knock-knock!
  Who's there?
Elvis!
  Elvis who?
Elvis help Santa!

Knock-knock!
  Who's there?
Enid!
  Enid who?
Enid some help with this knot.

    Knock-knock!
      Who's there?
    Escher!
      Escher who?
    Escher doorbell
    broken?

Knock-knock!
  Who's there?
Esther!
  Esther who?
Esther bunny!

    Knock-knock!
      Who's there?
    Stella!
      Stella who?
    Stella nother Esther bunny!

Knock-knock!
  Who's there?
Fido!
  Fido who?
Fido what you say, will you let me in?

Knock-knock!
Who's there?
Foreman!
Foreman who?
Foreman only—not
three or five!

Knock-knock!
Who's there?
Hank!
Hank who?
Hank you very much!

Knock-knock!
Who's there?
Hardy!
Hardy who?
Hardy a nice way to greet a friend!

Knock-knock!
Who's there?
Howie!
Howie who?
Howie forgets who I am every
time, I'll never know!

Knock-knock!
Who's there?
Hugh!
Hugh who?
Hugh loves ya, baby!

Knock-knock!
Who's there?
Irene!
Irene who?
Irene you going to invite
me in?

Knock-knock!
Who's there?
Isadore!
Isadore who?
Isadore locked or can
I just walk in?

Knock-knock!
Who's there?
Ishmael!
Ishmael who?
Ishmael in the mail box
for you!

Knock-knock!
Who's there?
Ivanna!
Ivanna who?
Ivanna come in and watch the game!

Knock-knock!
Who's there?
Jacket!
Jacket who?
Jacket the mall told me to come get you!

Knock-knock!
  Who's there?
Jeannie!
    Jeannie who?
Jeannie us is very rare,
you know!

Knock-knock!
  Who's there?
Jerome!
    Jerome who?
Jerome is so messy, I
can't even see the bed!

Knock-knock!
  Who's there?
Julie!
    Julie who?
Julie me no choice!

Knock-knock!
  Who's there?
Keith!
    Keith who?
Keith me even though I
have no fwont teef!

Knock-knock!
Who's there?
Kenny!
Kenny who?
Kenny come out or can't he?

Knock-knock!
Who's there?
Laurel!
Laurel who?
Laurel catch up with you eventually,
so you might as well give up!

Knock-knock!
Who's there?
Leonard!
Leonard who?
Leonard every word you said!

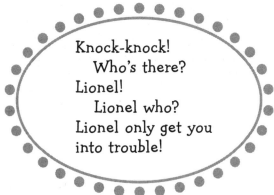

Knock-knock!
Who's there?
Lionel!
Lionel who?
Lionel only get you
into trouble!

Knock-knock!
Who's there?
Lisa!
Lisa who?
Lisa know who my friends are!

Knock-knock!
  Who's there?
Louis!
  Louis who?
Louis been telling me for
a long time that I should
meet you!

Knock-knock!
  Who's there?
Luke!
  Luke who?
Luke out—the sky is
falling!

Knock-knock!
  Who's there?
Mabel!
  Mabel who?
Mabel I'll come back later!

Knock-knock!
  Who's there?
Marcus!
  Marcus who?
Marcus coming along
later!

Knock-knock!
  Who's there?
Maria!
  Maria who?
Maria man that you love and
you'll always be happy!

Knock-knock!
  Who's there?
Midas!
  Midas who?
Midas well admit it, you
don't even know who I am!

Knock-knock!
  Who's there?
Miguel!
  Miguel who?
Miguel has left me! Help
me get her back!

Knock-knock!
  Who's there?
Milton!
  Milton who?
Milton cheese is really hot!

Knock-knock!
  Who's there?
Morrie!
  Morrie who?
Morrie talks, the sleepier
I get!

Knock-knock!
 Who's there?
Newman!
 Newman who?
Newman after a shower,
let me tell you!

Knock-knock!
 Who's there?
Oliver!
 Oliver who?
Oliver round the corner,
on the next block!

Knock-knock!
 Who's there?
Olivia!
 Olivia who?
Olivia friends, that's who! Surprise!

Knock-knock!
  Who's there?
Oswald!
  Oswald who?
Oswald my ice cream
so quickly, my head hurts!

Knock-knock!
  Who's there?
Rocky!
  Rocky who?
Rocky bye baby on the
treetop!

Knock-knock!
  Who's there?
Pushkin!
  Pushkin who?
Pushkin people around is
no way to make friends!

Knock-knock!
  Who's there?
Sally!
  Sally who?
Sally forth and get some
air with me!

Knock-knock!
  Who's there?
Sabine!
  Sabine who?
Sabine a long time
no see!

Knock-knock!
  Who's there?
Sarah!
  Sarah who?
Sarah nother way we
could do this?

Knock-knock!
  Who's there?
Samson!
  Samson who?
Samson is out here with
me. Where's Sam?

Knock-knock!
  Who's there?
Scott!
  Scott who?
Scott to be some kind of way out of here!

Knock-knock!
  Who's there?
Seamus!
  Seamus who?
Seamus already dark out!

Knock-knock!
  Who's there?
Selma!
  Selma who?
Selma lemonade on the corner
in front of the house!

Knock-knock!
  Who's there?
Sharon!
  Sharon who?
Sharon with people is how you make friends!

Knock-knock!
  Who's there?
Sheila!
  Sheila who?
Sheila only break your
heart, my friend!

Knock-knock!
  Who's there?
Shelby!
  Shelby who?
Shelby be sad she missed you!

Knock-knock!
  Who's there?
Sherwood!
  Sherwood who?
Sherwood like to come in and visit!

Knock-knock!
  Who's there?
Shirley!
  Shirley who?
Shirley you can't have forgotten my name already!

Knock-knock!
  Who's there?
Stephan!
  Stephan who?
Stephan it—we're
losing them!

Knock-knock!
  Who's there?
Tex!
  Tex who?
Tex one to know one!

Knock-knock!
  Who's there?
Therese!
  Therese who?
Therese got to be some other kind
of joke that you know!

Knock-knock!
  Who's there?
Thomas!
  Thomas who?
  Thomas something to tell you!

Knock-knock!
  Who's there?
Tyler!
  Tyler who?
Tyler bathroom and you'll never slip!

Knock-knock!
  Who's there?
Tyrone!
  Tyrone who?
Tyrone really fast!

Knock-knock!
  Who's there?
Wanda!
  Wanda who?
Wanda time is right,
you'll just know it!

Knock-knock!
   Who's there?
Watson!
   Watson who?
Watson the agenda for tonight?

      Knock-knock!
        Who's there?
      Woody!
        Woody who?
      Woody stop with all the knock-knocks!

3 * Moving and Grooving

Here's a little section that uses words ending with -er to create some knock-knocks. Check these out. Then, when you get the hang of it, see what you can come up with.

Knock-knock!
   Who's there?
Dancer!
   Dancer who?
Dancer is de same as de question!

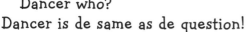

Knock-knock!
   Who's there?
Driver!
   Driver who?
Driver insane with all
these knock-knocks!

Knock-knock!
Who's there?
Filler!
Filler who?
Filler up—my cup is empty!

Knock-knock!
Who's there?
Flapper!
Flapper who?
Flapper wings and
quack like a duck!

Knock-knock!
Who's there?
Flasher!
Flasher who?
Flasher pearly whites at me!

Knock-knock!
  Who's there?
Hammer!
  Hammer who?
Hammer cheese—your choice!

      Knock-knock!
        Who's there?
      Jumper!
        Jumper who?
      Jumper rope with her—I'm going home!

Knock-knock!
  Who's there?
Pitcher!
  Pitcher who?
Pitcher hand out and we'll call it a deal!

      Knock-knock!
        Who's there?
      Poster!
        Poster who?
      Poster remember your
      friends' names!

Knock-knock!
  Who's there?
Settler!
  Settler who?
Settler stomach with a glass of warm milk!

Knock-knock!
  Who's there?
Shaker!
  Shaker who?
Shaker tail feather!

Knock-knock!
  Who's there?
Shaver!
  Shaver who?
Shaver breath—I'm not
convinced!

Knock-knock!
  Who's there?
Slipper!
  Slipper who?
Slipper my name and see
if she knows who I am!

Knock-knock!
  Who's there?
Trader!
  Trader who?
Trader warm house for
this cold porch!

4 * Door-to-Door Delivery !

Here you'll find some delicious knock-knocks that are sure to deliver. Knock-knocks about everything from turnips to coconuts and everything in between. Savor the flavor and enjoy these mouth-watering knock-knocks while they're hot!

Knock-knock!
  Who's there?
Apple!
  Apple who?
Apple on the door and it just came right off the hinges!

Knock-knock!
  Who's there?
Baker!
  Baker who?
Baker a cake. After all, it's her birthday!

Knock-knock!
  Who's there?
Beets!
  Beets who?
Beets me—I thought you might know!

        Knock-knock!
          Who's there?
        Orange!
          Orange who?
        Orange you glad I didn't say beets?

Knock-knock!
  Who's there?
Biscuit!
  Biscuit who?
Biscuit dressed and come
outside!

Knock-knock!
  Who's there?
Butcher!
  Butcher who?
Butcher hands up and
give me three cheers!

Knock-knock!
  Who's there?
Candy!
  Candy who?
Candy come out
and play?

Knock-knock!
  Who's there?
Cantelope!
  Cantelope who?
Cantelope—I'm already
married!

Knock-knock!
  Who's there?
Carrot!
  Carrot who?
Carrot all about my
opinion?

Knock-knock!
  Who's there?
Cauliflower!
  Cauliflower who?
Cauliflower by another
name and it still smells
as sweet!

Knock-knock!
  Who's there?
Coconut!
  Coconut who?
Coconut only delicious,
it's good for you too!

Knock-knock!
  Who's there?
Donut!
  Donut who?
Donut tell me you
forgot me!

Knock-knock!
  Who's there?
Eggs!
  Eggs who?
Eggs it to the left, please,
and no pushing!

Knock-knock!
  Who's there?
Ketchup!
  Ketchup who?
Ketchup before you get
left behind!

Knock-knock!
  Who's there?
Kipper!
  Kipper who?
Kipper silly questions to
yourself!

Knock-knock!
  Who's there?
Kumquat!
  Kumquat who?
Kumquat-ly and there'll
be no trouble!

Knock-knock!
  Who's there?
Liver!
  Liver who?
Liver die, it's up to you!

Knock-knock!
 Who's there?
Mango!
 Mango who?
Mango work in the
midday sun!

Knock-knock!
 Who's there?
Meaty!
 Meaty who?
Meaty your family
explains a lot about you!

Knock-knock!
 Who's there?
Mustard!
 Mustard who?
Mustard left my hat
behind!

Knock-knock!
 Who's there?
Olive!
 Olive who?
Olive my other friends
know who I am!

Knock-knock!
  Who's there?
Pasta!
  Pasta who?
Pasta cheese, please!

Knock-knock!
  Who's there?
Pudding!
  Pudding who?
Pudding yourself in
harm's way is foolish!

Knock-knock!
  Whos' there?
Rhubarb!
  Rhubarb who?
Rhubarb or her twin
sister?

Knock-knock!
  Who's there?
Salad!
  Salad who?
Salad a cold so
he sent me!

Knock-knock!
  Who's there?
Shallot!
  Shallot who?
Shallot least let me
in to tell you!

Knock-knock!
Who's there?
Sherbet!
Sherbet who?
Sherbet this'll be
a great evening!

Knock-knock!
Who's there?
Soda!
Soda who?
Soda first thing you have to
do is to remember my name!

Knock-knock!
Who's there?
Sushi!
Sushi who?
Sushi always drops me
off right here!

Knock-knock!
Who's there?
Thirsty!
Thirsty who?
Thirsty makes me knock,
then he forgets my name!

Knock-knock!
Who's there?
Turnip!
Turnip who?
Turnip the volume—
I can't hear the music!

5 * From Everywhere To Your Front Door

The world is a funny place. Trust me, I know about these things. I've been everywhere and let me tell you, the places are as funny as the names. No matter where you are, the town, state or country you're in is perfect fodder for your next knock-knock. So let these gems take you wherever you want to go and back again to your front door.

Knock-knock!
　Who's there?
Abyssinia!
　Abyssinia who?
Abyssinia the next time around!

Knock-knock!
　Who's there?
Canada!
　Canada who?
Canada silly questions
and just let me in!

Knock-knock!
  Who's there?
Castle!
  Castle who?
Castle never let me hear the end of this!

Knock-knock!
  Who's there?
Coal mine!
  Coal mine who?
Coal mine number and find out!

Knock-knock!
  Who's there?
Cuba!
  Cuba who?
Cuba is what you use on a pool cue!

Knock-knock!
  Who's there?
Everest!
  Everest who?
Everest with those
questions?

Knock-knock!
  Who's there?
Hannover!
  Hannover who?
Hannover the keys and
I won't have to keep
knocking on the door!

Knock-knock!
  Who's there?
Hawaii!
  Hawaii who?
Hawaii doing this
afternoon?

Knock-knock!
  Who's there?
India!
  India who?
India meantime, why don't
we play some cards!

Knock-knock!
  Who's there?
Iran!
  Iran who?
Iran and ran, but I couldn't
catch up with you!

47

Knock-knock!
Who's there?
Jamaica!
Jamaica who?
Jamaica mistake, you have to admit it!

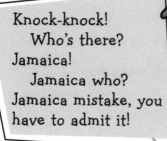

Knock-knock!
Who's there?
Kenya!
Kenya who?
Kenya give me a break, just for once!

Knock-knock!
Who's there?
Melbourne!
Melbourne who?
Melbourne on the same day as I was!

Knock-knock!
Who's there?
Missouri!
Missouri who?
Missouri loves company!

Knock-knock!
Who's there?
Ohio!
Ohio who?
Ohio you feeling any better?

Knock-knock!
    Who's there?
Russian!
    Russian who?
Russian around all day makes me tired!

Knock-knock!
    Who's there?
Scotland!
    Scotland who?
Scotland his football right on your doorstep!

Knock-knock!
  Who's there?
Sweden!
  Sweden who?
Sweden sour are my
favorite flavors!

Knock-knock!
  Who's there?
Tibet!
  Tibet who?
Tibet on the horses, you
have to go to the races!

Knock-knock!
  Who's there?
Tunis!
  Tunis who?
Tunis stuck in my
head—can you hear it too!

Knock-knock!
  Who's there?
Venice!
  Venice who?
Venice the party going to
start?

6 ✳ Sick Stuff

As I mentioned before, my doctoring is limited to knock-knocks, and laughter is the best medicine! Still, if these don't make you feel better, take two from the next section and call me in the morning.

Knock-knock!
    Who's there?
Bandage!
    Bandage who?
Bandage is about eighteen years old, isn't it?

Knock-knock!
    Who's there?
Coffin!
    Coffin who?
Coffin and sneezing out here!

Knock-knock!
  Who's there?
Disease!
  Disease who?
Disease the way you treat your friends?

Knock-knock!
  Who's there?
Exam!
  Exam who?
Exam good with bacon!

Knock-knock!
  Who's there?
Freeze!
  Freeze who?
Freeze a jolly good
fellow!

Knock-knock!
　Who's there?
Oiled!
　Oiled who?
Oiled people can't help it if
they have some hearing loss.

Knock-knock!
　Who's there?
Q-Tip!
　Q-Tip who?
Q-Tip me off to a good place to
play basketball around here?

Knock-knock!
　Who's there?
Snot!
　Snot who?
Snot my fault!

Knock-knock!
　Who's there?
Splinter!
　Splinter who?
Splinter arm until it stops
hurting!

Knock-knock!
Who's there?
Surgeon!
Surgeon who?
Surgeon the fourth floor
told me to come and ring
your bell!

Knock-knock!
Who's there?
Suture!
Suture who?
Suture self—be that way
if you want to!

Knock-knock!
Who's there?
Witch hazel!
Witch hazel who?
Witch hazel do you mean—
this one or that one?

Knock-knock!
Who's there?
Wound!
Wound who?
Wound you be my
neighbor?

7 * The Sweet Sounds Of Knock-Knocking

Ah, what could be sweeter than the sound of knock-knocks being delivered all across the land—happy doors being opened by happy people who then get happier hearing great knock-knocks. It's enough to make you smile and pick up an instrument—if you know how to play an instrument. Otherwise, put that thing down!

Knock-knock!
  Who's there?
Celeste!
  Celeste who?
Celeste time I'm going to tell you,
so try and pay attention!

Knock-knock!
  Who's there?
Didgeridoo!
  Didgeridoo who?
I didn't know you could yodel!

Knock-knock!
  Who's there?
Gong Gong!
  Gong Gong who?
Gong, Gong, gone!

Knock-knock!
  Who's there?
Guitar!
  Guitar who?
Guitar invitation to
come out and play?

Knock-knock!
  Who's there?
Harmonica!
  Harmonica who?
Harmonica and her
sister home?

Knock-knock!
  Who's there?
Mandolin!
  Mandolin who?
Mandolin look pretty!

Knock-knock!
    Who's there?
Organ!
    Organ who?
Organ let me in this time,
or should I just forget it?

Knock-knock!
    Who's there?
Treble!
    Treble who?
Treble with you is, you
never remember anything!

Knock-knock!
    Who's there?
Violins!
    Violins who?
Violins is never the answer—
let's talk about it!

Knock-knock!
    Who's there?
Xylophone!
    Xylophone who?
Xylophone with the right
number this time!

8 * Sports Snorts

Now it's time to take a crack at some sports knock-knocks. Knockle balls, if you will. So step on up and see how you do with these babies. But be careful—they're tricky and they play hard. So strap on your helmet, your gloves, and whatever else you need to enter the high-speed world of the sporting knock-knock.

Knock-knock!
  Who's there?
Archery!
   Archery who?
Archery tree has ripe
fruit on it now!

Knock-knock!
   Who's there?
Backstop!
    Backstop who?
Backstop hurting yet?

Knock-knock!
Who's there?
Biplane!
Biplane who?
Biplane or by boat, I told you I'd come!

Knock-knock!
Who's there?
Canter!
Canter who?
Canter sister come out to play for a while?

Knock-knock!
Who's there?
Catcher!
Catcher who?
Catcher before she leaves here and starts home!

Knock-knock!
Who's there?
Discus!
Discus who?
Discus it with me before you ask so many questions, why don't you?

Knock-knock!
Who's there?
Dumbbell!
Dumbbell who?
Dumbbell doesn't work—I've been out here forever!

Knock-knock!
Who's there?
Helmet!
Helmet who?
Helmet me and told
me to come over!

Knock-knock!
Who's there?
Homer!
Homer who?
Homer where the heart is!

Knock-knock
Who's there?
Hurdle!
Hurdle who?
Hurdle have to speak up,
I can't hear too well.

Knock-knock!
Who's there?
Mantle!
Mantle who?
Mantle me you have
free apples!

Knock-knock!
Who's there?
Mascot!
Mascot who?
Mascot a cold. You
don't have it, do you?

Knock-knock!
Who's there?
Miniputt!
Miniputt who?
Miniputt my books in
your bag again!

Knock-knock!
Who's there?
Pitcher!
Pitcher who?
Pitcher a ball and see
how she hits!

Knock-knock!
Who's there?
Pucker!
Pucker who?
Pucker a ball—whatever
you've got will do!

Knock-knock!
Who's there?
Racket!
Racket who?
Racket up to experience,
I suppose!

Knock-knock!
Who's there?
Skidoo!
Skidoo who?
Skidoo make you go
faster—you were right!

Knock-knock!
  Who's there?
Shortstop!
  Shortstop who?
Shortstop you from getting too hot in the summer!

Knock-knock!
  Who's there?
Shot put!
  Shot put who?
Shot put you in the
lead—nice going!

Knock-knock!
  Who's there?
Stockcar!
  Stockcar who?
Stockcar wagon is stuck
in the mud!

Knock-knock!
　Who's there?
Tennis!
　Tennis who?
Tennis when you said to come,
isn't it?

Knock-knock!
　Who's there?
Water wings!
　Water wings who?
Water wings good for on our model
airplane?

Knock-knock!
　Who's there?
Water skis!
　Water skis who?
Water skis doing on your feet
in the middle of winter?

Knock-knock!
　Who's there?
Yoga!
　Yoga who?
Yoga any idea how long
I've been out here?

9 ✳ Space Cadets on Your Porch

A h, space, the final frontier. Or was that TV? I can never remember. In any case, here are some knock-knocks that are out of this world. Well, unless they're still in orbit, in which case they're almost out of this world. You know what I mean.

Knock-knock!
Who's there?
Astronaut!
Astronaut who?
Astronaut that good for drinking soup!

Knock-knock!
Who's there?
Atmosphere!
Atmosphere who?
Atmosphere of the dark is a childish fear!

Knock-knock!
  Who's there?
Comet!
    Comet who?
Comet down a little
and I'll tell you!

Knock-knock!
  Who's there?
Cosmonaut!
    Cosmonaut who?
Cosmonaut here right
now, but if you'd like to
leave a message . . .

Knock-knock!
  Who's there?
Crystal!
    Crystal who?
Crystal me you make the
best cookies. Got any left?

Knock-knock!
  Who's there?
Jupiter!
    Jupiter who?
Jupiter feet near me one
more time, I'll scream!

Knock-knock!
  Who's there?
Krypton!
  Krypton who?
Krypton quietly into the
night....

Knock-knock!
  Who's there?
Lunar!
  Lunar who?
Lunar different than
ducks, right?

Knock-knock!
  Who's there?
Martian!
  Martian who?
Martian all day is only going
to make your feet hurt!

Knock-knock!
  Who's there?
Meteor!
  Meteor who?
Meteor new neighbor!

Knock-knock!
  Who's there?
Orbit!
  Orbit who?
Orbit of a space cadet yourself,
aren't you?

Knock-knock!
  Who's there?
Rocket!
  Rocket who?
Rock it on over, the big
dog is moving in!

Knock-knock!
  Who's there?
Satellite!
  Satellite who?
Satellite on in your window?

Knock-knock!
  Who's there?
Saturn!
  Saturn who?
Saturn your lunch
by mistake—sorry!

Knock-knock!
    Who's there?
Shuttle!
    Shuttle who?
Shuttle the windows—
it's going to rain!

Knock-knock!
    Who's there?
Solar!
    Solar who?
Solar what you have on
the bottom of your feet!

Knock-knock!
    Who's there?
UFO!
    UFO who?
UFO wonder if there's
life on other planets?

10 * Bundle Up and Stamp Your Boots

Who was it that said that clothes make the man? Well, clothes also make the joke!

Knock-knock!
   Who's there?
Ascot!
   Ascot who?
"Ascot what your
country can do
for you . . ."

Knock-knock!
   Who's there?
Blouses!
   Blouses who?
Blouses what the
wind does!

Knock-knock!
Who's there?
Bowler!
Bowler who?
Bowler best, but I'm still
going to win!

Knock-knock!
Who's there?
Button!
Button who?
Button on a bit of a
show, aren't you?

Knock-knock!
Who's there?
Collar!
Collar who?
Collar on the phone if
you want to talk to her!

Knock-knock!
Who's there?
Glove!
Glove who?
Glove is all you need!

Knock-knock!
Who's there?
Jacket!
Jacket who?
Jacket school said you were
awesome at football!

Knock-knock!
  Who's there?
Parka!
    Parka who?
Parka cross the street
is open—let's go!

Knock-knock!
  Who's there?
Pullover!
    Pullover who?
Pullover, would you?
I can't read this map!

Knock-knock!
  Who's there?
Pocket!
    Pocket who?
Pocket the other end of the ice rink,
so what are you doing over here!

Knock-knock!
  Who's there?
Sandal!
  Sandal who?
Sandal over my feet—
that's the beach!

Knock-knock!
  Who's there?
Slipper!
  Slipper who?
Slipper number under the door.

Knock-knock!
  Who's there?
Sneaker!
  Sneaker who?
Sneaker way out of the house
and meet me later!

Knock-knock!
  Who's there?
Sweater!
  Sweater who?
Sweater stay dry, it all depends on how hard you
work!

11 ∗ The Octopus's Garden

Ah, the deliciousness of fishiness. The water world is full of wonderful creatures, and they, in turn, are perfect for the knock-knock joke. Fish or fin, they are all wet and wild bait for our next round of knock-knocks. Get ready to go deep!

Knock-knock!
  Who's there?
Albatross!
  Albatross who?
Albatross-ed our ball
over your fence. May we
have it back?

Knock-knock!
  Who's there?
Anemone!
  Anemone who?
Anemone wouldn't knock,
so don't worry!

Knock-knock!
   Who's there?
Barracuda!
   Barracuda who?
Barracuda bit me in the woods!

Knock-knock!
   Who's there?
Canoe!
   Canoe who?
Canoe believe I'm back
again?

Knock-knock!
   Who's there?
Cod!
   Cod who?
Cod your cold, and now
my nose is running!

Knock-knock!
　Who's there?
Eel!
　Eel who?
Eel your cold by spending
the day in bed!

Knock-knock!
　Who's there?
Flounder!
　Flounder who?
Flounder sitting on your front
porch. Is she your sister?

Knock-knock!
　Who's there?
Grouper!
　Grouper who?
Grouper waiting at the park.
Are you coming or not?

Knock-knock!
　Who's there?
Seaweed!
　Seaweed who?
Seaweed already decided you'd meet
us here, so why are you surprised?

Knock-knock!
Who's there?
Halibut!
Halibut who?
Halibut you let me in and
we'll talk about it where
it's warm?

Knock-knock!
Who's there?
Herring!
Herring who?
Herring is your problem, not
memory—you don't listen to
anything I tell you!

Knock-knock!
Who's there?
Kelp!
Kelp who?
Kelp me! I can't swim!

Knock-knock!
Who's there?
Manatee!
Manatee who?
Manatee would really
warm me up right now!

Knock-knock!
Who's there?
Minnow!
Minnow who?
Minnow you're in there, so come
out with your hands up!

Knock-knock!
Who's there?
Oyster!
Oyster who?
Oyster and stir, but it
never turns into custard!

Knock-knock!
Who's there?
Pike!
Pike who?
Pike riding is my favorite
thing to do!

Knock-knock!
Who's there?
Puffin!
Puffin who?
Puffin up like that is not
going to make you look
any taller!

Knock-knock!
Who's there?
Seahorse!
Seahorse who?
Seahorse running at you,
you better sprint!

Knock-knock!
   Who's there?
Shellfish!
   Shellfish who?
Shellfish of you to forget my name!

Knock-knock!
   Who's there?
Skate!
   Skate who?
Skate at home, or should
I come back later?

Knock-knock!
   Who's there?
Snapper!
   Snapper who?
Snapper fingers twice and make a wish!

Knock-knock!
Who's there?
Tidal!
Tidal who?
Tidal the shoelaces together—
this is going to be hilarious!

Knock-knock!
Who's there?
Tortoise!
Tortoise who?
Tortoise out of the paper and
thought you might be interested!

Knock-knock!
Who's there?
Trout!
Trout who?
Trout be told, I've forgotten myself!

Knock-knock!
Who's there?
Tuna!
Tuna who?
Tuna piano, would ya? You're killing
me over here!

Knock-knock!
Who's there?
Urchin!
Urchin who?
Urchin you one last time
to reconsider!

Knock-knock!
Who's there?
Water!
Water who?
Water you doing wearing
my favorite sweater?

Knock-knock!
Who's there?
Whale!
Whale who?
Whale never get there if
you just stand around
asking questions!

12 ★ The Whole Kit and Kaboodle

Here's where we pull out all the stops and really let you have it. This is the big kahuna. This final section is where we lay it all on the line with a cornucopia of knock-knocks and let you pick your favorites from the bunch. There's everything in here from pencils to poppies and the kitchen sink, as well. Enjoy, and don't forget to breathe in-between!

Knock-knock!
  Who's there?
Argue!
  Argue who?
Argue coming out
with me or not?

Knock-knock!
  Who's there?
Basket!
  Basket who?
Basket in out of the sun, I'm
getting burned!

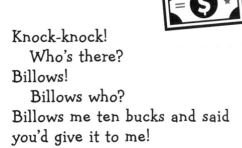

Knock-knock!
  Who's there?
Billows!
  Billows who?
Billows me ten bucks and said
you'd give it to me!

Knock-knock!
Who's there?
Cancel!
Cancel who?
Cancel lemonade without any lemons!

Knock-knock!
Who's there?
Cargo!
Cargo who?
Cargo right past your house every morning!

Knock-knock!
Who's there?
Casual!
Casual who?
Casual keep forgetting my name, I'm moving!

Knock-knock!
Who's there?
Center!
Center who?
Center a message I was coming!

Knock-knock!
Who's there?
Coolant!
Coolant who?
Coolant you have there; I can't wait to meet your uncle!

Knock-knock!
  Who's there?
Cotton!
  Cotton who?
Cotton the middle again!

Knock-knock!
  Who's there?
Curtain!
  Curtain who?
Curtain his brother said
you had my football!

Knock-knock!
  Who's there?
Daisies!
  Daisies who?
Daisies a man, but by night, he's a werewolf!

Knock-knock!
  Who's there?
Dawn!
  Dawn who?
Dawn by bay the air is
clear!!

Knock-knock!
  Who's there?
Denial!
  Denial who?
Denial is a river in
Egypt.

Knock-knock!
  Who's there?
Disaster!
  Disaster who?
Disaster be the worst day
I can remember!

Knock-knock!
  Who's there?
Element!
  Element who?
Element for us to wait
here for her—she said so!

Knock-knock!
  Who's there?
Exit!
  Exit who?
Exit on the spot and
we'll call it signed!

Knock-knock!
  Who's there?
Ferris!
  Ferris who?
Ferris fair, and since you
asked, I'll tell you!

Knock-knock!
  Who's there?
Hair!
  Hair who?
Hair you haven't been
feeling well!

Knock-knock!
  Who's there?
Heaven!
  Heaven who?
Heaven we met
somewhere before?

Knock-knock!
  Who's there?
Hey!
  Hey who?
Hey you, yourself and mind your
manners. I have a name, you know!

Knock-knock!
Who's there?
I-Ching!
I-Ching who?
I-Ching eyes and runny
nose? Must be allergies!

Knock-knock!
Who's there?
Island!
Island who?
Island my helicopter
on your roof!

Knock-knock!
Who's there?
Jewel!
Jewel who?
Jewel find out if you
open the door!

Knock-knock!
Who's there?
Lego!
Lego who?
Lego of the door and I'll
tell you!

Knock-knock!
  Who's there?
Maiden!
  Maiden who?
Maiden America—that's
where, not who!

Knock-knock!
  Who's there?
Major!
  Major who?
Major day by showing up,
didn't I?

Knock-knock!
  Who's there?
Marionette!
  Marionette who?
Marionette all of my lunch. Can I have some of yours?

Knock-knock!
  Who's there?
Mistake!
  Mistake who?
Mistake my leave of you!

Knock-knock!
  Who's there?
Mission!
  Mission who?
Mission you every
time you go away!

Knock-knock!
  Who's there?
Mister!
  Mister who?
Mister birthday party but
I got something for her!

Knock-knock!
  Who's there?
Mustache!
  Mustache who?
Mustache the cheese
so the cat won't find it!

Knock-knock!
  Who's there?
Nickel!
  Nickel who?
Nickel be here any
minute—let's go!

Knock-knock!
  Who's there?
Orchids!
  Orchids who?
Orchids are tougher
than your kids!

Knock-knock!
  Who's there?
Ottoman!
  Ottoman who?
Ottoman do what he
thinks is best?

Knock-knock!
  Who's there?
Pencil!
  Pencil who?
Pencil keep falling down
if you don't get a belt!

Knock-knock!
  Who's there?
Picture!
  Picture who?
Picture number out of a
hat!

Knock-knock!
  Who's there?
Police!
  Police who?
Police to finally meet you!

                    Knock-knock!
                      Who's there?
                    Pressure!
                      Pressure who?
                    Pressure face up against the
                    glass and you'll be able to tell!

Knock-knock!
  Who's there?
Radio!
  Radio who?
Radio not, here I come!

Knock-knock!
  Who's there?
Samurai!
  Samurai who?
Samurai should really
have called first!

Knock-knock!
  Who's there?
Say!
  Say who?
Who!

Knock-knock!
  Who's there?
Scold!
  Scold who?
Scold out here!

Knock-knock!
  Who's there?
Scolder!
  Scolder who?
Scolder out here
than I thought.

Knock-knock!
  Who's there?
Scooter!
  Scooter who?
Scooter self outta here
and play ball with me!

Knock-knock!
  Who's there?
Should hold!
  Should hold who?
Should hold acquaintance
be forgot . . .

Knock-knock!
Who's there?
Shutter!
Shutter who?
Shutter to think what your
memory must be like!

Knock-knock!
Who's there?
Shut-in!
Shut-in who?
Shut-in the door will
stop you falling out!

Knock-knock!
Who's there?
Smarty!
Smarty who?
Smarty at home?

Knock-knock!
Who's there?
Speckle!
Speckle who?
Speckle have to refresh
your memory!

Knock-knock!
Who's there?
Spell!
Spell who?
W-H-O!

Knock-knock!
Who's there?
Stranger!
Stranger who?
Stranger things have happened!

Knock-knock!
Who's there?
Tanks!
Tanks who?
Tanks for asking!

Knock-knock!
Who's there?
Teacher!
Teacher who?
Teacher my name, would you!

Knock-knock!
  Who's there?
Thumping!
  Thumping who?
Thumping tells me this isn't
your first knock-knock joke!

Knock-knock!
  Who's there?
Van!
  Van who?
Van I know, I'll tell you!

Knock-knock!
  Who's there?
Waiter!
  Waiter who?
Waiter you waiting for?

Knock-knock!
  Who's there?
Wallet!
  Wallet who?
Wallet the audience decide!

Knock-knock!
    Who's there?
Warrant!
    Warrant who?
Warrant you going to call
me when you got home?

Knock-knock!
    Who's there?
Who?
    Who who?
What are you, an owl?

Knock-knock!
    Who's there?
Winsome!
    Winsome who?
Winsome, lose some!

Index